£1·99

KT-484-696

The Challenge of Immigration – a Radical Solution

The Challenge of Immigration – a Radical Solution

GARY S. BECKER

WITH A COMMENTARY BY DIANE COYLE

The Institute of Economic Affairs

THE AUTHORS

Gary S. Becker

Gary S. Becker won the 1992 Nobel Prize in Economic Sciences 'for having extended the domain of microeconomic analysis to a wide range of human behaviour and interaction, including non-market behaviour'. He is Professor of Economics and Sociology at the University of Chicago. He is also the Rose-Marie and Jack R. Anderson Senior Fellow at the Hoover Institution; and a Research Associate of the Economics Research Center at the National Opinion Research Center. Gary S. Becker pioneered study in the fields of human capital, the economics of the family and the economic analysis of crime, discrimination, addiction and population. He is a founding member of the National Academy of Education, a member of the National Academy of Science and a fellow of the American Statistical Association, the Econometric Society and the American Academy of Arts and Sciences. He is also a member of the American Economic Association, of which he was president in 1987. In 1967, Gary S. Becker was awarded the John Bates Clark Medal, which is given once every two years to the most outstanding American economist under the age of 40. He was also awarded the National Medal of Science in 2000 for his work in social policy, and the Presidential Medal of Freedom in 2007, the highest civilian award in the USA. Gary S. Becker's current research focuses on human capital, the family and economic growth. He was a featured columnist for *Business Week* and co-author of the Becker-Posner Blog, which can be viewed at http://www.becker-posner-blog.com/.

Diane Coyle

Diane Coyle runs the consultancy Enlightenment Economics and is the author of *The Soulful Science* and *The Economics of Enough*. Diane is a visiting professor at the University of Manchester and has a PhD from Harvard University. She is a trustee of the BBC and has served on a number of other public bodies. Diane is currently a member of the UK's Migration Advisory Committee, but she has contributed to this monograph in a personal capacity.

FOREWORD

Immigration is a controversial subject among free-market economists. It is frequently the case that those who are well disposed towards a market economy and the free movement of capital are not in favour of free – or even freer – immigration. Tony Benn once made that very point about the former Conservative, and later Ulster Unionist, Member of Parliament Enoch Powell.

Various different reasons are given for this opposition to migration by supporters of otherwise free markets. Some fear cultural change; others feel that free-market arguments do not really apply to migration in an era of expansive welfare states; still others feel that the UK is densely populated already and migration would put pressure on house prices. In some cases, these arguments relate to the 'economics of second best' or the ordering of policy decisions. Those who oppose free migration because of the existence of welfare states, for example, may wish to dismantle those welfare states and then would welcome free migration. Those who worry about house prices might prefer a different approach to planning matters first.

Despite the existence of greater scepticism regarding the free movement of labour than regarding the free movement of capital, many free-market supporters nevertheless strongly favour liberalisation of immigration. It has been pointed out, for example, that the last era of globalisation brought much greater migration than the current era. Furthermore, despite the reservations expressed above, it is argued that migration benefits both recipient countries and the migrants themselves.

Gary S. Becker is not a libertarian when it comes to migration. In the 2010 IEA Hayek Memorial lecture given at Church House, Westminster, on 17 June 2010, and reproduced in this monograph, he suggests that migration should be limited. Rather than bureaucratic controls being introduced, however, he suggests using the price mechanism to limit immigration. In the authoritative and lucid style that typifies Gary S. Becker, he presents a well-argued case that his proposal would ensure that migrants who entered the country under his scheme would be those who provided the greatest net benefit.

Indeed, Gary S. Becker's proposal provides us with a coherent framework within which we can try to resolve the debates between those who want a restrictive and those who want a liberal immigration policy. Those who want a liberal policy in principle would support a very low or zero fee. Those who use economic arguments for restricting immigration would be able to consider the reduction in taxation that the fee would facilitate in the context of the other economic costs and benefits of immigration.

The EU context is perhaps a little different. There is free migration within the EU in any case. Also, Gary S. Becker's proposal tends to provide an incentive for permanent rather than temporary migrants. Temporary migration to the UK is common, however, and perhaps even regarded as desirable. This does not undermine the concept of the fee in principle but it might suggest some practical differences if the scheme were applied in the UK.

Diane Coyle, a member of the Migration Advisory Committee

(though writing in a private capacity), provides an introduction to the UK context and a commentary on Gary S. Becker's proposals. In particular, she brings in non-economic issues that might be important and which, she believes, might make Gary S. Becker's proposals unacceptable in practice in the UK.

Both the lecture itself and the critique are important contributions to the debate. The debate was launched by Gary S. Becker's visit to the IEA, which was accompanied by a significant amount of media coverage and political discussion of his proposals. The IEA is delighted to continue to promote the case for market-oriented solutions to economic and social problems by the permanent publication of the lecture, the question-and-answer session and the commentary.

PHILIP BOOTH

Editorial and Programme Director, Institute of Economic Affairs
Professor of Insurance and Risk Management,
Cass Business School, City University
February 2011

controlling economic migration than the use of quotas and
other bureaucratic systems of control.

- Even a fee of $50,000 would allow people on relatively low
earnings to enter the USA if there were skill shortages. Given
the level of wage differentials, such a fee could be paid back in
a few years or in a decade or so.

- Certain categories of migrant might be allowed to benefit
from a loans system to enable them to pay the fee over a
period of years. This could operate rather like a student loans
system in higher education.

- One advantage of using a fee rather than administrative
controls would be that illegal immigrants would have a strong
incentive to regularise their status – and would be allowed to
do so legally. Such people would have to pay the required fee
but would then be free to choose much more remunerative
occupations. As such, the use of the price mechanism
in migration policy could alleviate the scourge of illegal
immigration.

FIGURES AND TABLES

1 THE CHALLENGE OF IMMIGRATION – A RADICAL SOLUTION
Gary S. Becker

Introduction

It is a great pleasure to be here and to speak at the Hayek lecture. I attended Professor Hayek's seminars – I always think of him as Professor Hayek – at the University of Chicago. They were evening seminars and very stimulating. He had leading figures at the University of Chicago from all disciplines: Enrico Fermi from physics, Sewall Wright, the great biologist, Milton Friedman and others who spoke before them. I also knew quite well Arthur Seldon and Ralph Harris, the two founder directors of the Institute of Economic Affairs. I met them primarily through the Mont Pèlerin Society meetings in which they were both active and in which I became active after a while. So it is a double pleasure to be here giving the Hayek lecture at the Institute of Economics Affairs with my fond memories of Hayek, Lord Harris and Arthur Seldon.

The topic this evening is immigration. This is clearly a very controversial subject in Great Britain, but also in the United States, in Japan and in continental Europe. It is a controversial subject in Mexico too, though they think of it in a different way from the way we think of it in the United States, but it is still a big subject. Of course, there are many other countries around the world where it is important too.

Despite the controversy over immigration, immigration

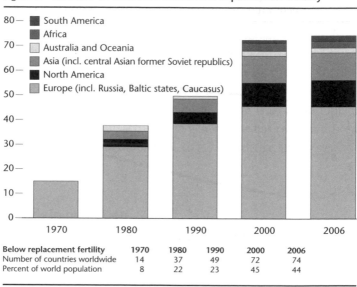

Figure 2 **Number of countries with below-replacement fertility**

Below replacement fertility	1970	1980	1990	2000	2006
Number of countries worldwide	14	37	49	72	74
Percent of world population	8	22	23	45	44

in which I have been interested and which I could spend another few lectures discussing. Perhaps I will come back and give another lecture on that subject at some point because it's such a fundamental change in the world as we look forward. Almost a half the world's population now live in countries with below-replacement fertility.

So given those forces – low incomes, combined with low birth rates that are mainly in the richer countries in the world – you see a great pressure to move. And we can see what happened to world immigration. The figures in Table 1 show net immigration. They look at, for a given region, how many people are coming in relative to how many people are leaving and net these two figures out. For some purposes, gross immigration – that is the number of people coming in – might be a better measure, but the data in Table 1 are net. There has been a large growth since 1970 in the amount of world net immigration and you can see that the growth in Europe is very substantial and that the figure for North America is also very substantial. Some regions have had a growing deficit – people are leaving these regions. Other regions have been fairly neutral in that immigrants are roughly balanced by emigrants.

Table 1 **Immigration for world and by region, 1980–2010[1]**

Net immigration, '000s

	1970	1980	1990	2000	2005
World ($\geqslant$0 countries)	1,542	2,612	3,456	3,886	4,657
Europe & Central Asia	–120	255	473	649	1,670
North America	514	715	1,268	1,743	1,353
Middle East & North Africa	–1	94	36	–51	–64
Sub-Saharan Africa	–110	–68	–225	57	–319
East Asia & Pacific	167	–189	286	–344	–341
South Asia	–99	–349	–361	–571	–636
Latin America & Caribbean	–363	–456	–720	–763	–1,157
UK	–50	–11	6	99	190
US	333	635	1,090	1,596	1,135

Current immigration policy

So, on the one hand, you have the substantial pressure of people wanting to come to the richer countries. On the other hand, you have strong opposition in richer countries to unlimited immigration. The USA, until the early twentieth century, basically had unlimited immigration – anybody could come and millions upon millions of people did come. There was continuing opposition to

---

1   The figure shown for the world is essentially total movement – that is, the sum of all the figures for countries which have positive net migration.

that, particularly towards the end of the nineteenth century, and eventually we passed, in the 1920s, very restrictive laws.

All countries now have very restrictive laws. What is interesting is that the criteria used are very different. In Table 2, we can see net immigration to different countries and I select out a few, including the UK and the USA, and the criteria used. You might think that work (allowing people to come in because they have skills and so on) would be the major criteria for allowing people to immigrate. But, for a lot of political economy reasons, that is not so.

The criteria for the USA are rather different from those for other countries. In the USA, only a very small proportion enter for work-related reasons. Most come in for family reunification and for humanitarian reasons. The fact that the USA is allowing people in for family reunification and for humanitarian reasons is perfectly fine and understandable, but that there is such a small fraction entering the country for work-related reasons is surprising.

If you look at other countries the reasons for entry vary a lot. Canada has a somewhat larger fraction and the UK a much larger fraction for work-related reasons.[2] So there is a considerable variation in the reasons by which immigrants can attain access. But, generally speaking, all the rich countries have limits on who can come and they use a variety of criteria.

---

2 Editorial note: it is likely to be the case that this larger fraction for work-related reasons in the EU countries is because migration is essentially uncontrolled within the EU. There are still substantial restrictions on out-of-EU migration for work-related reasons.

Table 2 **Approaches to controlling immigration**

	Number (000)	% work	% family	% humanitarian	% other
UK	343.2	53.2	31.8	8.9	6.0
Germany	216.0	70.3	23.3	2.8	3.6
Italy	204.3	53.2	41.7	3.1	2.0
France	169.0	26.1	59.0	4.4	10.5
Canada	251.6	22.1	60.8	17.0	0.1
US	1,266.3	5.6	70.3	17.1	7.0

Some of my libertarian friends – with whom I have a lot of sympathy in most areas of policy – have said to me that we should just go back to US policy in the nineteenth century and allow unlimited immigration. Look at all the great value we have obtained from immigrants, they argue. I am second to no one in believing that immigrants have been a huge source of value for most countries, and certainly for the USA. My wife is an immigrant, my parents were immigrants and there's hardly an American, if you go back only a few generations, where you do not find immigrant ancestors. But the world is very different now from the way it was at the end of the nineteenth century and the beginning of the twentieth century. The differences really come down to the role of government and to the welfare state. It is human nature – responding to incentives – to move to a country and get a lot of benefits, such as welfare benefits. It is true that not everybody will move for those benefits but a significant fraction of people will move to try to take advantage of welfare benefits and other economic goods provided by a government. So the welfare state makes it very unattractive to go back to the immigration policies that the USA had in the late nineteenth century.

There is also another aspect to the immigration debate. Even if you had rules – for example, limiting how soon immigrants can collect welfare benefits, and it would be very hard to implement such rules politically – governments are big and immigrants become voters and they influence the outcomes of elections. Therefore, there is much concern about knowing the political affiliations of immigrants and how they will influence government spending and push for this type or that type of spending. So for those two reasons it is not realistic – it is not even desirable – to go back to the model of unlimited immigration, however much value immigrants have contributed to different societies.

So the question one has to address is, given this practical situation, what should we do? Should we follow the present policies that are a mixture of interest-group-based limitations? For example, the United States has 'H1B immigrants' who can come in as skilled workers and stay for up to six years. Many of them are from Asia. This does not seem very threatening, even though it does not seem optimal. Yet the US Congress has pushed the quota back so that only about seventy thousand H1B immigrants can come in every year. This means that usually by the end of January the quota is filled – it is already filled for this fiscal year.

Many more people want to immigrate than can come in. Such approaches do not seem to be the right way to go about controlling immigration.

Illegal immigration is also worth mentioning. Limits on entering legally lead people to come illegally instead. The USA has a large number of illegal Mexican immigrants and the UK has a large number of illegal immigrants from various countries outside the EU, where entry is restricted.

A radical policy proposal

So, how can we improve the system? First, I accept the fact that most immigrants add a lot to countries, that they are conscientious, that they are hard-working, that they do unpopular jobs and add skills. Immigration may also bring some negative features. Crime rates are often higher among immigrants and there are some other problems that you are all familiar with. So the question that I have tried to think about is how can one maximise and preserve the advantages of having many immigrants and reduce the disadvantages? I have a very simple proposal. You might say it is naively simple. The proposal is that governments should sell the right to immigrate. The government should set a price each year and anyone would be accepted, aside from obvious cases such as potential terrorists, criminals and people who are very sick and who would be immediately a big burden to the health system. But aside from these cases, you would allow anybody to immigrate who could make the payments. No country has ever adopted such a policy. The US policy, in the nineteenth century, where anybody could immigrate, had this system with a zero price. But no country has ever really adopted a system of allowing anybody to immigrate if they can pay a given price. You might say that one reason nobody has adopted the system is because it is a dumb proposal. I am going to try to convince you that it is not a dumb proposal, that it makes a lot of sense and that it meets a lot of the objections from people opposed to large numbers of immigrants. The idea also caters to the people who would like to see more immigrants. I believe, for example, that the USA should allow more immigration. So it is not perfect but it will be a major improvement over the present system.

Who would be attracted to immigrate?

I will come a little later to what the entry fee might be. For illustration, at this point, I am going to pick a number. Suppose you set the fee at $50,000 for the USA, and a related figure for the UK, what would happen? The first question to ask is this: who would be most willing to pay that price? You can think of different groups who may be willing to pay. It would include those who were more skilled, because the gain from moving from a poor country to a richer country for skilled persons is substantially greater than the gain from moving from a poor country to a rich country for the less skilled. If you look at the skilled people coming from India or China, they gain about $20,000 to $30,000. For example, a graduate from the Indian Institute of Technology, which is a very fine place to be trained as an engineer, would increase his income by a minimum of $30,000 a year in the United States and by a somewhat smaller but still substantial figure in the UK. In this case, the cost of $50,000 for entering the country would be repaid very rapidly – within two years for most of them.

So, skilled immigrants would clearly be attracted by this system. The young would also be attracted for obvious reasons; they would have a longer time to collect the benefits. Young people who have a lot of new ideas, who are energetic, who want their families to improve in the future and so on would be attracted because they would gain a lot.

The third category of people who gain is also important and sometimes neglected. A country really wants immigrants who make a commitment to the country they are entering. Some immigrants will be disappointed, they will go back. But a country hopes those who stay want to make a commitment to the culture of the country they are entering, even if they also preserve some of their own cultures; and countries want the children of immigrants to make a commitment too. Such immigrants would find a fee system most attractive, and they would be willing to pay the most since they expect to stay the longest. So the first three main categories of immigrants that would be attracted by a fee system would be skilled people, young people and those who want to make a commitment to the country. They would be the ones who would be most willing to pay a large fee.

Dealing with opposition to immigration

The opposition to immigration has often claimed that immigrants get a free ride. They come in, so they argue, make use of free health services and the educational system and get other benefits. That is why opponents want to reduce immigration. In the system that I am proposing immigrants are not getting a free ride as they are paying for the right to enter and are adding to tax revenue. The UK and the USA and many other countries, as a result of the financial crisis, are in a situation where government revenue is an important issue. Governments are running large deficits. Under the policy I am proposing, immigrants would contribute revenue as well as receive some benefits. It should be added that most immigrants under the proposed system would generally work, be younger and more skilled, so their use of welfare benefits is often going to be minimal. Others will use the benefits, but they will also have contributed the fees. The revenue from the fee will not necessarily eliminate hostility to immigration but it will reduce this hostility. That is another important factor.

Illegal immigration

Illegal immigration is an important problem in many countries, even in Japan. Japan does not encourage immigration and has almost zero net legal immigration in any year, but it has many illegal immigrants. When my wife and I were in Japan not that long ago there were lots of complaints about people entering on tourist visas from the Philippines and from China and then staying on to work.

Immigrants come illegally because they cannot enter legally. Some people who are in a country illegally, such as in the UK, the USA or Germany, will reason that if they became legal immigrants by paying the entry fee they would have much better opportunities than illegal immigrants. Illegal immigrants can work but they are limited in the type of jobs they can have; they are in the underground economy pretty much entirely. We know from studies that the underground economy generally has low-skilled, lower-paying jobs, because a firm using many skilled workers really cannot function effectively being underground. This is why many illegal immigrants may well convert themselves to legal status by paying the fee. Not all of them would do that, of course, but those who want to make a long-term commitment to the country where they live are likely to do so. The fee approach would not eliminate the illegal immigration problem by any means but it would moderate, possibly substantially, the amount of illegal immigration. The illegal immigrants who want to make a commitment, who want their children to have opportunities, and who are most skilled, are most likely to convert themselves to legal status.

Loans for immigrants

People naturally would wonder about the plight of poor immigrants who cannot afford to pay the entrance fee. I do not want to exclude poor immigrants: particularly the poor ambitious immigrants who want to benefit not only themselves but also their children. These people are willing to work hard and save a lot because they take a long-run perspective. You want to encourage such immigration. It would be a foolish policy if those immigrants could not come. One has to think creatively about mechanisms by which we can help poorer immigrants finance a fee of, say, $50,000.

One approach is similar to a student loan programme. Student loans help mainly poor students finance their higher education and they pay loans back over a number of years. We could have an immigration loan programme. Immigration loans would enable poorer immigrants to invest in human capital in the form of moving to a country that offers them more opportunities. It would be analogous to student loans in many ways. Although the immigrants would have to be the ones indirectly paying the fees for immigration, they might finance their loans by making contracts with companies that pay the fees directly for them. In return, an immigrant could commit to working for the company for a certain number of years. If an immigrant decides to move to another company, he would have to repay the loan at that time (or have the new company repay the loan).

Such systems already help immigrants finance their education. Take, for example, Brazil – many students from Brazil have studied at the University of Chicago in economics and business. The Brazilian government has a programme whereby they finance the education, say at Chicago, for a student but the student has to make a commitment to come back and work for a number of years in certain specified activities (for example, either at a central bank or a university). If they do not do this they can repay the loan: they are given this option. That is similar to what you might have in the case of immigration. A company might help immigrants finance their loans, but if the immigrants go to work elsewhere they would repay the loan themselves or have their new employers help finance their loans. There is much flexibility once you start thinking along these lines; there are lots of ways by which poor individuals who are immigrating would not be excluded from paying entrance fees, and indeed, they could participate fully.

The practicalities

So how would the proposal work? First, of course, one has to determine a price, which would depend mainly upon two variables: how many immigrants a country wants to admit (that would be a decision that voters would have to make); and how the number of applicants would vary with price. If the number of applicants did not vary much with price, a country would get more revenue and not many fewer applicants by setting a higher price. If the number of applicants varied a lot with price, a country would have to take that into account in setting the entrance fee. These two factors would help determine the entrance fee.

I have made some rough calculations for the United States, because I know the data for the United States better, but you can easily substitute other numbers for Great Britain. The USA has been admitting about one million legal immigrants a year. The number of illegal immigrants is not known although there are various estimates. One question is, what equilibrium price would lead to one million immigrants wanting to come here legally? At a zero price many more than one million immigrants would want to come to the USA every year – probably the USA could get three million or more immigrants if they were allowed in at a zero price. That is how much excess demand there is. Let us suppose that a price of $50,000 would attract one million immigrants. That price would yield $50 billion a year in revenue. Since the USA has a big government deficit, $50 billion annually will not eliminate this deficit but it is a significant sum. At a 5 per cent interest rate it has a present value of roughly $1 trillion. With this revenue the opponents of immigration might decide that maybe immigration is not such a bad idea.

Perhaps the equilibrium fee would be higher than $50,000. Why do I say that? Think of how much many immigrants earn by coming to the UK or the USA compared with how much they would earn if they stayed where they are, whether it is India, China, Pakistan or elsewhere. As I mentioned before, IIT graduates from India would increase their income annually by maybe $30,000 a year. Obviously these are graduates of a very high skill level, but in less than two years they would pay their $50,000 fee. They could borrow the money and pay off the loan quickly. They would have a lot of money left over and be adding a lot of value to a country with their skills.

Of course, people with lower skills would gain much less from coming to the USA. But even an unskilled worker can make much higher wages in the USA than they can make in Pakistan or Mexico – which is the biggest source of immigrants to the USA. The gains to these migrants are substantial – several thousand dollars a year: maybe five to ten thousand dollars for an unskilled worker because the pay is so much better in the USA. So even an unskilled worker could pay off a loan quite quickly. My guess is that more than one million immigrants would come each year to the United States at a price of $50,000. Hence the revenue potential is great, but the main purpose of the proposal is not simply to raise revenue. It is to provide a criterion by which a country can select immigrants who have many advantages to the country they come to that go far beyond the fees they pay in terms of skills, youth, commitment, and so on.

Many technical details have to be worked out. Some people have argued that companies should buy the right to immigrate for their foreign employees. I think it is better to let individuals buy the right to immigrate rather than putting it in the hands of companies. A company may help an individual migrate but the responsibility should be in the hands of individuals, even if they decide to contract with companies.

One also has to take into consideration immigrants who come with children and spouses. I would pay a lot more for my spouse to come in than I would for myself, but not everybody would make that judgement! Moreover, a country might want different fees according to skill level. Still, it is better to start with a simple system and then introduce various complications. That is what I did in this lecture.

Conclusion

My conclusions are simple. Men and women in many parts of the poorer world want to immigrate to rich countries, particularly the UK, the USA, Germany and Japan. Many arbitrary rules are used to limit the number of immigrants allowed in. There is what we call in economics an excess demand for the right to immigrate because countries set various rules to ration entry.

When companies have excess demand for their products (for example, there may be greater demand for cars than there is supply of cars) companies raise the price of their products. In recent years the reverse has been true. There is a greater supply than demand for cars and companies have lowered prices – they offer zero per cent financing and various other discounts. This is the way markets operate. Think of immigration as a market. There is excess demand to come to many rich countries. If you use the market concept, the price is too low and countries should raise the price to come in. These are really the essentials of my proposal. The government should look for a price that equilibrates the desired number of immigrants with the number that want to enter.

One might think that by doing this a country will get a bad type of immigrant. In fact, it will get the better sort of immigrants for the most part. It will get the young, the skilled and those who have the greatest commitment to the country. Also, many illegal immigrants will pay the fees to convert themselves to legal status. So a country can have its cake and eat it too. The country gets the revenue, and the better sort of immigrants. It seems to me to be a win-win situation.

There is always political and intellectual opposition to new ideas, but I hope that when the concept of immigration fees spreads, and when the difficulties of present immigration policies become more and more apparent, countries will begin to contemplate using prices to restrict immigration by charging immigrants for the right to enter.

2 QUESTIONS AND DISCUSSION

Graham Smith: Given that the starting point for calculating the price is still that the government has to decide how many immigrants it wants to admit, is it not at least possible that a government that is attracted by a scheme of this sort would argue that it can avoid all the difficulty of trying to calculate an equilibrium price by setting a quota and auctioning the quota? Now if you see your proposal as preferable to that, how would you go about persuading a government of that?

Gary S. Becker: Well, you know, they are very much related proposals and I do not really have strong preferences for one or the other. You can think of starting with quantity and seeing what price you can get or you start with price and you think of quantity, and they are fundamentally very closely related. Think of the following comparison – you can either put a tax on carbon emissions or you can set a quota and sell the quota or give the quota away, and under various conditions they are equivalent ways of dealing with the same problem. These are basically the same system; you auction off the quota and you get the feedback from the demand at the price at which potential immigrants are willing to pay and maybe next year you set a higher or lower quota. And similarly the comparable issue would be, with the system I am proposing, that they set a price. Maybe they get less demand than they would like or they get more people who are willing to pay that price and the following year they will raise the price because they can attract the number they are seeking to get at a higher price. So they are equivalent methods, I do not have strong opinions about which one would be better.

Male speaker: One thing that instantly attracted me to the plan is the fact that you, with perhaps George Borjas, are probably the most reviled economists among the left wing, which obviously makes it a great selling point. But how do we sell it to those economists and the political economists, the politicians? As you say, how on earth do we sell this plan; is it incremental or is it, just, here's $50 billion dollars to plug your hole? Which one is the better argument for them?

Gary S. Becker: Well, I am a believer in the division of labour. All of my career I have tried to come up with ideas and I leave it to the IEA and other think tanks and other people to do the selling. I do

write a little bit for the popular media and I
have a blog and I have written for *Business Week*
for nineteen years, but I feel my contribution
is to come up with the ideas. Still, how would
it be sold? I think it would be sold basically
by think tanks and others picking up this
idea and putting it in a way that would be
more attractive politically. All ideas have to
be implemented politically and put in a way
that makes them more attractive politically.
Even my great teacher and great friend Milton
Friedman at one time had the view that all he
had to do was come up with the right answer
and the politicians would jump to accept it.
Well, he learned over the years that is not
how things work. The way I think things
work is that, when a policy gets bad enough,
people look around, including people in the
political sector, and ask what is a better way
of addressing this problem? So when we
had airline regulation, that was leading to a
tremendous number of inefficiencies; people
began to write in the academic world and in
the think tank world and in the popular media,
that the regulations were counterproductive.
Then the system collapsed and when something
collapses it always comes as a surprise. Airline
regulation collapsed actually under President
Carter, who was no particular friend of free
markets. But then reform came. So I think you

need the idea to be picked up by people who are specialists and good at putting these ideas in ways that are more appealing to the general public and to people in politics. And is that possible? Yes, it is easy to state the principles of charging for the right to immigrate. I do not believe I used a single technical term in anything I said this evening. I could write down equations to do all that and express it in a more complex way, but you do not have to do so. One can do it with simple language, and simple programmes are much easier to sell. So I think it is sellable. It is not going to happen tomorrow, but one has to look ahead when thinking about ideas. And whether it might happen in five years, ten years ... If it happened in ten years I would really feel great – I mean, that is a short horizon for the way ideas percolate throughout the system.

Nicholas C: Good evening, my name is Nicholas. I was wondering, is the USA not actually already experimenting with this de facto in a couple of ways? One is, I believe, that you can get a green card either by investing $0.5 million or $1 million into building a business. Secondly, you can also buy your way into the USA if you get into university: and we all know that it is usually quite expensive to pay for university over there. So on the basis of that could we compare the impact of at least these two experiments, let's say, that are happening in the USA with other countries where such ways of buying one's way into the country do not exist?

Gary S. Becker: The fraction of individuals who come to the USA by buying their way in is minute: those who offer, say, two or three hundred thousand dollars to come in have to invest it in certain industries ... That is also true in Canada. It is a tiny fraction of the total, so we are not using the system I proposed. You might say the USA uses it in terms of students coming to study in the United States. Yes, it is somewhat easier to immigrate if you come to study in the USA, but I have many former students who have had to go back because they could not convert their student visas into permanent visas. A student cannot automatically stay. One of the crimes of the US policy is that it gets all this talent coming, mainly for graduate studies, and they are not allowed to automatically stay – perhaps by buying their way in. The USA can attract tremendous numbers of able students. Two-thirds of the graduate students in the economics department at Chicago University are now from outside the United States. A significant fraction of them go back, partly because they have good opportunities elsewhere. That is fine, but they also go back partly because the USA makes it difficult to stay. That is the bad part, that is what my system would solve.

Eric Benson: My question is about default. So it would seem to me that a lot of people may not be able to pay this fee – particularly in the USA or Europe, where it is fairly expensive. What happens if they cannot? Do they go home, do they become economic refugees?

Gary S. Becker: Well, it is a good question and I have thought a little bit about that problem. The way I think the system would work would be that people would have to make a down payment and they could borrow the rest. Let us say the fee is $50,000. You could not borrow the whole $50,000. You would have to make some down payment – maybe $5,000 or $10,000. There is an expression we use in the United States, I don't know if you use it here in Great Britain: you have skin in the game. So you have some skin in the game by putting that money down. So default, yes, there will be some people defaulting; do you send them back, do you redo the loans? With student loans in the United States you cannot default. Government naturally always give themselves an advantage when it comes to default possibilities. You can default on a lot of other things but you can't default either on your taxes or on your student loan. Now you may de facto default by just not paying but you cannot go bankrupt and discharge your student loan. So I would think the analogy with student loans would be the way I would attack that problem. There will be some difficult cases that you are going to have to deal with, whether you send them back the way we send illegal immigrants back or do something else. That would have to be worked out, but one possibility is that you send them back if they defaulted on their loan.

Barry M-C.: Professor Becker, my name is Barry Macleod-Cullinane. I am an elected local politician, so some of what you're saying is of real interest because here in London we see a lot of people who are smuggled into the country: particularly from China and Far Eastern countries. They often end up working in sex-trade occupations because they pay traffickers to get them into the country. They are locked out of the normal market and this sounds like a way that actually would lift people out of that situation, solving a lot of problems for politicians. Also it would remove the 'people traffickers' that are blighting so many people's lives. Have you actually looked at that aspect of your proposals?

Gary S. Becker: I have looked a little bit at it. I am glad you have raised that question. I looked at it not in the British context but in the US context. There is a lot of smuggling from Mexico into the United States so it would be a similar sort of smuggling. The smugglers are called mules: these are the guides who get paid to smuggle these people in. I had a student once who did a paper on what the pay was for these mules and how it varied with different economic circumstances. And yes, a lot of people come in under awful conditions and there have been examples where people have died being smuggled in and so on. These people would be put out of business – or at least mainly put out of business – if my proposal went through. I wouldn't say 100 per cent out of business but they would be mainly put out of business. If I get smuggled in, I have to pay for this, and not a small amount by a Mexican's standards. Then if I am caught I am thrown out again. So some people have come across four or five times. If you add up what these people are paying it is a lot of money. If they were to enter and pay the legal fee up front they could get good jobs and earn a lot more, and that would do away with most of the business of smuggling. Nature abhors a vacuum, and that is as true in the economic sphere as elsewhere. You have rationing, you get people going into business finding ways around the rationing, and that is what these people do. Unfortunately they often do it in very unattractive ways, bringing people in for prostitution, and there are lots of other problems. I am not saying that this problem is going to be 100 per cent solved but I think my proposal will help considerably.

Jonathan Wise: I have two questions. Do we not risk pricing out of the market non-economic contributors such as artists, writers, teachers, nurses, etc? And, as a corollary to the point raised above, is there not a loophole (unless the constitution is changed) in that there is an incentive to have children so that they automatically become US citizens and thereby can get in through the back-door family allowance?

Gary S. Becker: Well, the children can be citizens. That does not automatically make their parents citizens. The constitution says that anybody born in the United States is a citizen of the United States. It does not say that makes their parents citizens. Their parents still have to go through regular devices to become citizens of the country. I have given some thought to the issue of what you do when people want to bring in their spouses or their children. Should they be allowed to bring them in at the same price? Probably they should not. If you bring in more people you have to pay more – maybe not proportionately but you would have to pay more. So I don't think that is a difficult problem – I think it could be solved. On the issue of artists and the like, that is more complicated. There will be some fields where immigrants are offering more of what we call non-pecuniary benefits. But most of the people in the occupations you mentioned, including a lot of artists who come in, would be well able to pay this price. This is also the case with nurses. We have a lot of nurses from Jamaica in the United States; they do so much better in the United States in terms of earnings than they do in Jamaica. We would get more nurses rather than fewer because at the moment we ration how many of these nurses can come in. This is also the case with artists. It is nice to think of the artist as indifferent to money and working for the sake of being creative. I believe some artists are like that and you might lose some of them. How do they get in under present circumstances? It is difficult for them to get in at present. A lot of artists would see better opportunities, not only in terms of selling art but in terms of working at art schools and finding other artists to associate with. They may therefore still see it as beneficial to enter.

Richard Olsten: I am interested in the direction of the welfare system. Would you see a need for restrictions on access to the welfare system or do you assume that effectively the people who are going to be coming in would be very keen to stay well away from welfare? And if that's the case would there be a significant saving for government, which you would add on to your $50 billion?

Gary S. Becker: Well, some people might pay to come in to take advantage of the welfare system although they

would pay a significant sum to do that. At the
moment, people come in, they take advantage
of the welfare system and they have not paid
anything to come in. On the other hand, most
of the immigrants who would come in under
the system I am proposing would be people
who would not need the welfare system, at
least for quite a while, because they would
be skilled workers, young workers and so on.
Maybe if they became unemployed they would
take unemployment compensation. So there
would be two factors mitigating the potential
problems. On the one hand, if people came to
take advantage of the welfare system at least
they would have paid a considerable sum to
take advantage of it. Secondly, the type of
people who would be attracted would be willing
to pay that sum because they would mainly be
people who would not need to take advantage
of the welfare system because they would be
earning a lot, would be relatively healthy and so
on.

A. Treacher: I am wondering whether there is a presumption
in your solution that permanent migration is
necessarily better than temporary migration.
If so it seems to fly in the face of changing
trends in migration where people might go for
a few years to a country, study, do some work
and then go back. This is particularly so with
regard to migration from developing countries

where we think of it as being a good thing that people come to other countries and experience other cultures and go back. Your policy might massively exacerbate brain drains and other related problems.

Gary S. Becker: Well, I do believe, on the whole, that people who come permanently are more valuable to a country. I am thinking here of the receiving country's perspective, not from the original home country's perspective. Permanent migrants are more valuable and they make a commitment to the country. It is better to have citizens in the country who are making a commitment to the country than people who are only coming for a short while and do not get involved in learning anything about the constitution or the other laws of the country and who do not want their children to really participate in learning about the country. So, on the whole, you are right that this is my underlying assumption. Now this does not mean that everybody who comes will stay for ever. Take somebody coming from India. They might come for ten years – which is impossible now – they earn a lot; they pay the $50,000; they have some surplus left over; they can take any job they want; they come in legally; and then they decide to go back, perhaps because economic opportunities have improved in India. You know, some costs are sunk. That is a basic principle of economics. Such a person would ask, looking ahead, what is better for me? Is it my opportunities in India now or my opportunities to continue in the United States? Some people might go back and that's fine. I have no objection to that. But for the most part you would get people making a commitment. I think mainly you want people who are making a commitment to the country rather than people who are coming temporarily.

Linda Whetstone: I wanted to ask about immigration for humanitarian reasons. I am sure you will have thought about it and there would have to be some other provision for that, surely.

Gary S. Becker: Clearly humanitarian reasons are significant but they account for quite a small number of migrants. If you look at the data that I presented they were a small fraction of the total immigrants. If we go back to the figures I presented, 17 per cent of those coming to the USA came in for humanitarian reasons; 9 per cent in the case of the UK; 3 per cent in Germany; and a little over 4 per cent in France. So, for most countries, it is not a major factor and clearly you might want to make exceptions for humanitarian reasons. But you have to be sure: you have to be sure they really are humanitarian reasons. A lot of people claim refugee status and it is not really justified. They claim that if they went back to their country of origin, they would be in trouble. For those people you are really confident about, you would have some exceptions. Maybe you would have a lower price because even those coming for humanitarian reasons will work and earn money. So you are getting to a smaller and smaller subset: those people coming for truly humanitarian reasons who maybe are too old to earn anything. You can make some exceptions for that group, but it is going to be a tiny fraction of the total coming in.

3 COMMENTARY ON *THE CHALLENGE OF IMMIGRATION – A RADICAL SOLUTION*
Diane Coyle[1]

Professor Gary S. Becker is renowned for the application of economic analysis to aspects of life previously thought to be outside its bounds. His proposal for reform of immigration policy is in the same tradition. It is widely accepted that economic ambition motivates would-be migrants, and the framework for policy has in many countries increasingly involved an assessment of immigrants' economic contribution to the host country. Taking the next step of extending economic logic to making migration policy market based, however, is unlikely to win instant acceptance, for reasons I discuss below. First, however, I will set out the UK context.

The UK context

Net migration into the UK is a phenomenon of globalisation. Globally, numbers of migrants have increased as a proportion of the population, and the UK is not the only country to have experienced the phenomenon. Other major recipient countries include the USA, Australia, Ireland (until its severe economic downturn) and Switzerland.

There are inconsistencies between different sets of statistics,

---

1   Although the author is a member of the UK's Migration Advisory Committee (MAC), the commentary reflects her personal view and not the view of the Committee.

but all paint the same picture of a marked upward trend in both gross and net immigration to the UK from the mid-1990s.[2] This levelled off in 2008 owing to the economic downturn, but remained at a high level in early 2010. The accession of new member countries to the EU in 2004, combined with the UK's decision not to impose temporary restrictions on workers from the newly joining countries, sustained the upward trend and also changed the composition of inward migrants. The proportion arriving from EU as opposed to non-EU countries increased. People in the new wave of migrants were less likely to settle in London and instead spread more widely around the UK. The new migrants were also somewhat less likely than previous migrants to find work in skilled jobs, although the broad pattern has been that migrants take either low-skill or high-skill jobs, rather than jobs in the middle of the skills distribution.

The biggest single category of today's UK immigrant stock consists of people from other EU states. Over the twenty years to the mid-2000s the numbers of people from black African countries, India, Pakistan, Bangladesh and old Commonwealth countries also grew, while the stock of people from black Caribbean countries, Ireland and also African-Asians declined. The immigrant population is slightly younger on average, at 38, than the resident population. The median age on arrival in Britain of a new migrant is 22, so the 'typical' immigrant is young (although this varies greatly between different groups).

Perhaps most relevant for understanding labour market impacts is the educational attainment of the typical immigrant.[3]

---

2   A detailed description of the trends can be found in MAC (2008) and MAC (2010).

3   The following draws on MAC (2008) and Dustmann and Glitz (2005).

is on labour market impacts and specifically on ensuring that the composition of migration in the future would emphasise the skill level of immigrants. The dual aim is to increase the average skill level of new immigrants (and hence of the workforce available to UK employers overall) by making entry easier for skilled workers (and, at present, not permissible for unskilled workers); and to increase the likelihood that immigrants' skills are complementary to those of the existing workforce by making entry easier for people working in occupations requiring skills in short supply in the UK.

In 2006 the UK government published its plans for a system for managing immigration, broadly modelled on a system already in use in Australia. The rationale was to identify and admit those immigrants who would have the highest level of skills to contribute to the UK; and also to make the system more transparent and objective, although it remains complex. The new system, introduced in stages from mid-2008, consists of five tiers: tier 1 for the highly skilled; tier 2 for other skilled workers with a job offer in shortage occupations; tier 3 for a limited number of low-skilled workers to fill specific shortages (temporarily suspended); tier 4 for students; and tier 5 for temporary workers. The system applies only to non-EEA citizens, as EEA citizens have the right to work in the UK anyway (with the exception of transitional restrictions for two new member countries, Bulgaria and Romania). Especially with tier 3 suspended, the new system leans heavily towards skilled immigrants and this tendency has increased with its increasing restrictiveness.

For those highly qualified and well-paid individuals qualifying to enter under tier 1, the system is not prescriptive about what particular gaps in the labour market they should be filling. For tier 2, however, replacing the old work permit system, permission to enter depends on holding specific skills required in a list of shortage occupations for which there is no sensible alternative for employers other than non-EU immigrant workers. The first such list of occupations was drawn up by the Migration Advisory Committee (of which I am a member) and published in September 2008.

The occupations on the list are winnowed out from the enormous range of occupations in the economy in a three-stage analysis. The following three questions are asked. Which occupations are skilled (originally defined as requiring the equivalent of NVQ level 3 or higher, subsequently raised to level 4)? In which of these is there a shortage of labour (assessed using a range of indicators)? And in which of these shortage occupations is there no sensible alternative to migrant workers? The current list covering occupations ranging from civil engineers to ballet dancers is based on assessment of an enormous amount of evidence relating to each of the three 'Ss', skilled, shortage and sensible, and also on a certain amount of judgement, especially with regard to the 'sensible' criterion.

Economists who believe that markets adjust to reduce disequilibria (such as skills shortages) find the MAC's task philosophically uncomfortable. Indeed, drawing up a list of specific occupations has a faint musty whiff of 'manpower planning' exercises, which have not been undertaken since the 1970s. In practice, however, rather than assuming that labour markets do not adjust and the task is to compensate for that, the MAC's work has focused on the alternative ways in which the markets can adjust, with a preference for increasing the skills available in the UK population.

Assessing whether or not there is a shortage in a given occupation is challenging, as simple economic theory tells us that wages could be expected to adjust to equalise supply and demand in a given labour market. Clearly a shortage in this 'static' sense cannot last long. The static model is an oversimplification of actual labour markets, however, which are dynamic and subject to adjustment costs; increasing labour demand can lead to a shortage that persists for some time if it takes time for the labour market to adjust. The speed of adjustment of labour supply and wages therefore becomes an important consideration. In practice the MAC uses a wide range of indicators of 'dynamic' shortages such as vacancy rates, earnings growth, unemployment and employer surveys. It should be noted, however, that the existence of shortages, or their prevalence in particular occupations, will change over time, and perhaps quite rapidly depending on the speed of adjustment.

Of most interest, however, is the 'sensible' question. What is sensible depends on both the underlying aims and the different means of attaining those aims. 'Sensible' depends on the scope for employers to adjust to use alternatives other than (non-EU) immigrant labour. The question speaks directly to the extent to which immigrant labour is complementary to or a substitute for domestic labour supply; and also to the extent that there is structural adjustment in the economy changing the nature of the demand for labour.

In practice, the MAC asked:

- What are employers' alternatives to using migrant labour – can they increase wages; make production less labour intensive; relocate to lower-labour-cost countries; change their product/service mix to be less labour intensive overall;

train the existing (potential) workforce? MAC also asked over what time period these things can be done.

- Would using migrant labour damage incentives to upskill the domestic workforce, even if it was a realistic and sensible short-term response to a shortage?
- How would the employment of immigrants affect investment, innovation and productivity growth – especially in specific sectors where maintaining international competitiveness is vital – for example, financial services, software?
- How would it affect the wider UK labour market and economy, if at all?

The points-based system has been in operation only for a short period, coinciding with the downturn, but in its first year there was a reduction in the number of work-related migrants.

This system – and certainly the MAC's interpretation of its task – is focused on increasing the selectivity of the policy, ensuring that immigration is complementary to the existing skill structure of the UK workforce and does not disincentivise upskilling. The aim has been to identify areas of shortage seriously hampering employers in their current activities, where immigrants will complement the UK-based labour force without losing sight of the need for education and training to improve the skills of the existing workforce. Immigration policy cannot reverse-engineer the education and training system, but should surely not undermine the incentives for improving skills.

The new government intends to go further, however. There will be unavoidable uncertainty in implementation. For example, it is impossible to predict with confidence the extent to which employers will switch to EU from non-EU migrants, or whether some will offshore their activities if they cannot use immigrant workers in the UK. As I write, the final details of the mechanisms it will choose to restrict net migration substantially have not been announced. The options on which the government consulted, however, did not include anything like Professor Becker's proposal of selling the right to immigrate; it intends to continue to use administrative methods of setting quantities and selecting skilled migrants. So I turn now to why politicians and voters might be resistant to using price, rather than quantities, to limit immigration.

Political economy of a market mechanism for immigration

One of the obvious objections to using the price mechanism to select immigrants is that many will not be able to afford to pay upfront, but might nevertheless be valuable members of the host workforce. Professor Becker proposes a government loan scheme to advance such people the money upfront and collect repayments. This, of course, involves additional administration and cost in itself. There are also many migrants who might never earn enough to repay a large amount. Those who staff the teaching, health service and social care sectors would be among them. So would most of those working in the performing arts. It might seem an attractive scheme for bankers and corporate lawyers, in other words, but not for 'ordinary' immigrants.

Professor Becker suggests that with a loan scheme many would-be migrants could anyway afford to foot the cost. This seemingly practical objection and practical response starts to take us, I think, to the deeper reason why Professor Becker's proposal is not immediately attractive. It is that there is a dimension of fairness, an ethical dimension, to the issue of immigration which is not addressed by the purely economic arguments.

It becomes obvious that economics is not the whole story when you consider that there is certainly no professional consensus among economists for 'free migration' in the same way that there is a consensus for 'free trade'. It is a fundamental principle in economics, however, that free trades between individuals deliver the best outcomes, in the absence of significant externalities. This is why market economies create prosperity: people are able to apply resources, including their own labour, to the most productive uses. Just as free trade of goods is a mutually advantageous exchange, so, too, the freedom of movement to work should lead to better outcomes. Within national boundaries this is uncontentious. Nobody, for example, would advocate limiting internal migration, which in every country has long taken the form of people moving to work in the big cities.

Yet every leading economy limits international migration, as Professor Becker points out. The very wealthy can move freely, but the great majority is restricted by various administrative mechanisms. There are circumstances in which people (although not economists) prefer quantitative rationing to price mechanisms, and those are circumstances in which fairness is felt to trump efficiency. These circumstances can differ between countries and cultures. Many Britons believe healthcare should be rationed through the NHS, to which all should have comparable access. Most would agree that sales of organs should be prohibited in favour of the donor system. Many Americans would disagree with the first proposition and some even with the second. Across countries, however, there would be widespread agreement that in emergencies or wartime non-price allocation mechanisms should trump market mechanisms, even at the cost of inefficiencies and the emergence of black markets – and it is true that illegal immigration certainly forms a particularly nasty black market.

Professor Becker does in fact address the question of illegal immigration, and it is fair to ask whether a market-based system would help reduce this, and its associated miseries. It is of course the prohibition which creates the black market, and it is possible that the scope for paying for entry directly – rather than paying a trafficker – would reduce illegal flows. Applying economic logic, that might depend on the price that prevailed for entry in Professor Becker's market scheme, and on the alternatives in the countries that illegal migrants were leaving. But this seems to me an empirical question which is not easy to answer.

Even if I am right that a popular 'fairness' instinct of the kind I have discussed applies to immigration, Professor Becker does us a useful service in making us ask ourselves why permission to immigrate should not be auctioned to the highest bidders. His logic would apply to the desire, discussed above, for migration policy to select immigrants who complement, rather than substitute for, the existing UK workforce: those people who expect to receive a wage premium for the skills on entering the UK are most likely to bid successfully for permission to enter through a market mechanism.

His lecture does not, however, address the underlying rationale for migration limits. He argues for either setting a price to induce the desired quantity of immigration, or setting a quota and auctioning places. He also expresses a strong preference for permanent migrants, and does not discuss what happens when people want to leave the UK; but this is a serious impracticality – especially in the UK context. In 2009, 567,000 long-term migrants came to the UK and 371,000 people left the UK (including British,

EU and non-EU nationals, with more than half non-EU by origin). Over time, both gross inflows and outflows have risen, reflecting in large part the globalisation of the economy and the increasing likelihood that people – especially if skilled – will spend several years working overseas.

I would also have liked to see Professor Becker address the question of the economic case for the quantity that is the target of his policy. He notes that all countries impose limits but does not help us understand what a desirable limit would be. There are social welfare arguments that help address this question. Modern migration since the mid-1990s has broadly speaking coincided with increased employment and real wages in both host countries and in sending countries. As such, it is a reasonable starting point to assume that mutually beneficial exchanges are indeed taking place. Government intervention to prevent a voluntary exchange usually demands a justification. Free markets are the best (even if imperfect) mechanism for increasing welfare and interventions should tightly focus on externalities and flaws in the market mechanism. Freedom of choice matters in economics and it matters in terms of morality as well.

This takes us to one important rationale, more often implicit than explicit, for an interventionist migration policy. This is that identity matters when it comes to moral obligations – many people would argue that we have the strongest moral obligations to those who are closest to us. It would be widely accepted that policymakers in the UK should seek to ensure that people already living in the UK have adequate opportunities to gain skills and compete on reasonably equal terms for jobs, and that this aim should have a higher ranking in terms of social welfare than the well-being of those who are currently not living and working here.

The native-born who are unemployed or badly paid should in theory respond to market signals of dynamic labour shortage, such as wage premia. But it is clear that weaknesses in the education system and dysfunctional social norms impair domestic adjustment in response to these market signals. As long as there are people who have poor job prospects owing to long-term failures in the education system or in the welfare system, we should perhaps support them, and place that obligation ahead of the economic welfare gains that would arise from leaving employers to make a completely unconstrained choice about which individuals they can hire.

This is a valid social preference, one that would clearly command support at the ballot box. Immigration restrictions, however, are not the most direct way to support UK-resident individuals with poor life prospects: education policies and social reforms are needed. Employers cannot substitute a quickly trained but badly educated local worker for a foreign-born worker in jobs that require anything but the most basic skills, so they will in practice make other substitutions instead, as discussed above – for example in their use of capital, or in the mix of products and services they offer, or by 'offshoring'.

So immigration policy can achieve effectively more specific aims – including matching immigrant skills better to current shortages in order to maximise complementarities between the UK-born and foreign-born workforces; and raising the average skill level of workers available to UK employers, with the potential for productivity and knowledge spillovers to benefit all of their workforce and the wider economy. Supplementary aims of the policy could also include limiting local congestion in demand for housing or public services; and ensuring the immigration system is clear, predictable and fair. Other targets, however, such as improving the level of education and skills in general in the UK population, will be assisted only indirectly though immigration limits.

The policy debate does not always distinguish the economic, the social welfare and the distinct moral arguments about migration. Professor Becker's emphasis on the economic dimension usefully highlights the fact that there are separate dimensions to the discussion, if only through a lack of traction for his specific proposal in policy circles. If, however, purely economic arguments are to form the basis for the efficient selection of migrants given a desired quota or limit, they surely also ought to form the basis for calculating an optimal limit too. Not even such a distinguished economist as Professor Becker has yet given us the means by which to do so.

References

Dustmann, C. and A. Glitz (2005), *Immigration, Jobs and Wages: Theory, Evidence and Opinion*, London: Centre for Economic Policy Research.

Dustmann, C., F. Fabbri and I. Preston (2007), 'The impact of immigration on the British labour market', *Economic Journal*, 115.

MAC (2008), Migration Advisory Committee report: *First recommended shortage occupation lists for the United Kingdom and Scotland*, London: COI, http://www.ukba.homeoffice. gov.uk/sitecontent/documents/aboutus/workingwithus/ mac/first-lists.

MAC (2010), *Limits on Migration: Limits on Tier 1 and Tier 2 for 2011/12 and supporting policies*, London: COI, http://www. ukba.homeoffice.gov.uk/sitecontent/documents/aboutus/ workingwithus/mac/mac-limits-t1-t2/.

4 A REJOINDER
Gary S. Becker

I would like to thank Dr Coyle for her valuable observations on the structure of UK immigration, and the nature of the points system now being used, and for her comments on my proposal to sell the right to immigrate. I have a few brief reactions.

Her discussion of the points system clearly shows its intrinsic weaknesses. No government or private body is capable of determining which occupations need additional members and which do not. This is for markets and the forces of supply and demand to determine. As Dr Coyle indicates, the points system is manpower planning, and such planning has had a very bad record, partly because of the politics involved in determining which occupations are experiencing a 'shortage' of members. I indicate in my lecture that, among many other advantages, selling the right to immigrate would automatically select immigrants into occupations that pay well, including psychic benefits. This gives the most meaningful definition of 'shortage'.

Dr Coyle raises three possible objections to this market approach. She indicates that no government at present, including the new UK government, is considering selling rights to immigrate. Of course, I agree, but unfamiliar ideas do not take hold immediately. I believe that, as the difficulties of using other approaches to limit the number of immigrants become more obvious, support will grow for using a market-type approach.

Dr Coyle asks whether the desire for 'fairness' is a major obstacle to serious consideration of auctioning off the rights to immigrate. While fairness is a vague term, I do not see why an auction system is less 'fair' than a system that decides which immigrants are acceptable by their occupations, ethnicity or the other criteria that are typically used. Why is the UK's points system fairer when it excludes ambitious immigrants because they do not have the skills that the UK government deems more valuable?

Finally, Dr Coyle criticises my discussion because I do not specify how many immigrants should be admitted under the auction system. This is a fair question, but one that is not easily answered under any proposal to select immigrants, including the auction system. I believe the case for limiting the number of immigrants is mainly based on the large growth in government during the past 70 years. When they become citizens, immigrants can vote on welfare, other entitlements and on all other government policies. Their votes affect everyone. The magnitude of these effects on others, which economists call 'externalities', is the main intellectual justification for control over immigration.

Yet it is not easy to determine how many immigrants would be optimal, given these externalities, and also the benefits that immigrants bring. One strength of the proposal to sell the right to immigrate is that it forces governments to confront the trade-off between the prices to be charged and the number of persons willing to immigrate at these prices. As that trade-off gets analysed, a consensus might emerge on how many immigrants should be admitted.

Fortunately, we can more readily solve a much simpler but still highly relevant question. If the number of immigrants were kept constant at present levels, what immigration fees would lead to that same number of immigrants? To maintain the same number of immigrants, it is only necessary to estimate the demand to immigrate as a function of the cost of immigrating, a much more easily answered question than the broader issue of how many immigrants to accept.

ABOUT THE IEA

The Institute is a research and educational charity (No. CC 235 351), limited by guarantee. Its mission is to improve understanding of the fundamental institutions of a free society by analysing and expounding the role of markets in solving economic and social problems.

The IEA achieves its mission by:

- a high-quality publishing programme
- conferences, seminars, lectures and other events
- outreach to school and college students
- brokering media introductions and appearances

The IEA, which was established in 1955 by the late Sir Antony Fisher, is an educational charity, not a political organisation. It is independent of any political party or group and does not carry on activities intended to affect support for any political party or candidate in any election or referendum, or at any other time. It is financed by sales of publications, conference fees and voluntary donations.

In addition to its main series of publications the IEA also publishes a termly journal, *Economic Affairs*.

The IEA is aided in its work by a distinguished international Academic Advisory Council and an eminent panel of Honorary Fellows. Together with other academics, they review prospective IEA publications, their comments being passed on anonymously to authors. All IEA papers are therefore subject to the same rigorous independent refereeing process as used by leading academic journals.

IEA publications enjoy widespread classroom use and course adoptions in schools and universities. They are also sold throughout the world and often translated/reprinted.

Since 1974 the IEA has helped to create a worldwide network of 100 similar institutions in over 70 countries. They are all independent but share the IEA's mission.

Views expressed in the IEA's publications are those of the authors, not those of the Institute (which has no corporate view), its Managing Trustees, Academic Advisory Council members or senior staff.

Members of the Institute's Academic Advisory Council, Honorary Fellows, Trustees and Staff are listed on the following page.

The Institute gratefully acknowledges financial support for its publications programme and other work from a generous benefaction by the late Alec and Beryl Warren.

Other papers recently published by the IEA include:

The Legal Foundations of Free Markets
Edited by Stephen F. Copp
Hobart Paperback 36; ISBN 978 0 255 36591 8; £15.00

Climate Change Policy: Challenging the Activists
Edited by Colin Robinson
Readings 62; ISBN 978 0 255 36595 6; £10.00

Should We Mind the Gap?
Gender Pay Differentials and Public Policy
J. R. Shackleton
Hobart Paper 164; ISBN 978 0 255 36604 5; £10.00

Pension Provision: Government Failure Around the World
Edited by Philip Booth et al.
Readings 63; ISBN 978 0 255 36602 1; £15.00

New Europe's Old Regions
Piotr Zientara
Hobart Paper 165; ISBN 978 0 255 36617 5; £12.50

Central Banking in a Free Society
Tim Congdon
Hobart Paper 166; ISBN 978 0 255 36623 6; £12.50

Verdict on the Crash: Causes and Policy Implications
Edited by Philip Booth
Hobart Paperback 37; ISBN 978 0 255 36635 9; £12.50

The European Institutions as an Interest Group
The Dynamics of Ever-Closer Union
Roland Vaubel
Hobart Paper 167; ISBN 978 0 255 36634 2; £10.00

An Adult Approach to Education
Alison Wolf

Hobart Paper 168; ISBN 978 0 255 36586 4; £10.00

Taxation and Red Tape
The Cost to British Business of Complying with the UK Tax System
Francis Chittenden, Hilary Foster & Brian Sloan
Research Monograph 64; ISBN 978 0 255 36612 0; £12.50

Ludwig von Mises – A Primer
Eamonn Butler
Occasional Paper 143; ISBN 978 0 255 36629 8; £7.50

Does Britain Need a Financial Regulator?
Statutory Regulation, Private Regulation and Financial Markets
Terry Arthur & Philip Booth
Hobart Paper 169; ISBN 978 0 255 36593 2; £12.50

Hayek's *The Constitution of Liberty*
An Account of Its Argument
Eugene F. Miller
Occasional Paper 144; ISBN 978 0 255 36637 3; £12.50

Fair Trade Without the Froth
A Dispassionate Economic Analysis of 'Fair Trade'
Sushil Mohan
Hobart Paper 170; ISBN 978 0 255 36645 8; £10.00

A New Understanding of Poverty
Poverty Measurement and Policy Implications
Kristian Niemietz
Research Monograph 65; ISBN 978 0 255 36638 0; £12.50

Other IEA publications

Comprehensive information on other publications and the wider work of the IEA can be found at www.iea.org.uk. To order any publication please see below.

Personal customers

Orders from personal customers should be directed to the IEA:
Isha Kacker
IEA
2 Lord North Street
FREEPOST LON10168
London SW1P 3YZ
Tel: 020 7799 8907. Fax: 020 7799 2137
Email: ikacker@iea.org.uk

Trade customers

All orders from the book trade should be directed to the IEA's distributor:
Gazelle Book Services Ltd (IEA Orders)
FREEPOST RLYS-EAHU-YSCZ
White Cross Mills
Hightown
Lancaster LA1 4XS
Tel: 01524 68765. Fax: 01524 53232
Email: sales@gazellebooks.co.uk

IEA subscriptions

The IEA also offers a subscription service to its publications. For a single annual payment (currently £42.00 in the UK), subscribers receive every monograph the IEA publishes. For more information please contact:
Isha Kacker
Subscriptions
IEA
2 Lord North Street
FREEPOST LON10168
London SW1P 3YZ
Tel: 020 7799 8907. Fax: 020 7799 2137
Email: ikacker@iea.org.uk